a psalm for us

a compilation of spoken-word poetry and short
stories written and performed by Reyna Biddy

all artwork by Sara Faber ♈

for whomever this plants peace in..

a psalm for us

Reyna Biddy

Andrews McMeel
PUBLISHING®

Also by Reyna Biddy

I Love My Love

for: mark spears

i wanted to write a book about sadness, because it
only made sense. i wanted to talk about all the
things i've been through, so i could show people
how i fell apart. i wanted to let people in on my
depression, but you wouldn't let me. you let me
know how even though that's what makes me
beautiful..
that's - what makes me special.
my mistakes. my flaws. my lows.
you said, i'm one of the few who knows how to turn
their aches into something beautiful.
and—that's what makes me beautiful.

"people crave beautiful things,
people crave beautiful beings,
and that's why people crave you."

"write about love. write about new life.
write about better days. write about how,
if there's a will, there will always be a way."
so i will.
i thank you
for holding my head up, for holding my hand tight,
for holding me down,
when most needed.

- *opening letter* -

before all else i want to say thank you..
to you. whoever is reading *A Psalm for Us* in this
moment. i cannot express how blessed i feel to be
able to share this piece of material with you. when i
say i am the epitome of a "work in progress" i truly
mean it. over the past two years i've had to fail,
learn, and grow, in order to realize so many things
about, not only the world around me, but also, the
infinite worlds that live inside of me. i've had to
learn to differentiate between what deserves my
energy and what all deserves to be beneath, (and/
or) behind me. i've had to learn about all the things
that fulfill me and everything that, mostly, leaves me
empty. i've had to wonder, often, about whether or
not i have an addictive personality. and.. over time
i've found that, more likely than not, i don't—i'm
just a fiend for things that don't suit me well. i
make habits out of what destroys me.. and distance
myself from anyone or anything that adores me.
i subconsciously run from people who try to save
me.. in hopes that, maybe, they'll chase me. maybe
i'm just crazy. i'm still working on staying put. for so
long i've run toward temporary comfort.. and away
from anything that might have seemed permanent.
up until now—i've spent my time swaying.. from
one fragmented affair to another. i've had to work
on welcoming consistency. i've had to become a
lot more understanding that genuine people work

this way. people who genuinely care for your well-being.. usually, stay around. i'm still learning the meaning of "forever." i've had to figure out why it's so effortless that i pull out, yet, so hard for me to stay. i've had to force myself to stay long enough to learn myself better. i've had to figure out why a lot of the joy that i have is accompanied by deep-rooted sadness. i've had to find where that melancholy lies at night then comfort it. i've had to revisit the past so i could pick up the parts of me that i've wanted nothing more than to simply abandon. still, there are many parts, within me, i have yet to make peace with. i'm still trying. i'm still growing. it literally took months of social detachment for me to learn how to "find" myself. somewhere between *I Love My Love* and today.. i lost "me." in the midst of falling in love with the person i was, and am still, becoming.. i fell in love with someone else and put "me" on hold. i finally loved how it felt to be in love with a person who wanted nothing other than to love me—and only me. who had eyes for no one other. i still find myself trying to comprehend that. i still find myself wondering. i still find myself straying. solitude helped me realize that i'm really good at starting things.. it's just the "finishing" part that i'm almost incapable of. every day i work at getting better. i'd like to think that every day i'm becoming a better lover. every day i'm working on "becoming"

more. i'm working on discipline. i'm trying to get
familiar with routines. i'm still trying to love the
things that love me. i'm still working on staying.
i'm working on paying closer attention. i'm trying
to hold on more often. i'm trying to hold on a tad
bit tighter. i'm still trying to rid myself of old habits.
i'm working on letting go of old ways. within these
past two years.. i've picked up numerous pens, i've
initiated countless material.. material i kept trying
to force myself to love.. but never did. i kept writing
half ass. i caught myself being a lot more afraid. a lot
more frightened to open up. a lot more frightened to
be vulnerable. a lot more cautious of hurting people.
i kept forgetting what it meant to write from the
heart. i kept forgetting my heart. i kept forgetting
how this all started. but i think now.. finally.. i've
got it. just bear with me. try your best to not only
be patient with me.. but with yourself, as well. just
like you.. i'm still figuring "this" all out. this thing
called "me." this thing called life. all i know for sure
is.. my purpose in it. i know for sure i'm here to help
you. i know for sure that if you're going through
heartbreak.. mine has probably ached more.. so i can
probably heal you. i'm going to be honest.. i really
just want to write more often. i want us to get to
know each other better. i want nothing more than to
grow with you. i wanna be a part of your growth. i
know i'm especially "known" for being honest.. but

i've definitely worked on being a lot more open this time around. i want to touch on sensitive topics.. and hopefully help you understand that you aren't alone. again, i want to do better. i want to spill out my heart with no boundaries. i wanna talk about the present just as much as i talk about the past. i wanna help you get past "this." this thing called pain. this thing called confusion. i wanna talk about the mistakes i've made.. i wanna talk about the choices i've made. i wanna talk about the things i'm still struggling with.. alongside the lessons i've learned thus far. i wanna be transparent. i want, more than anything, for you to pick up parts of me. i want you to understand "this" better. this thing called "us." this thing called "you." *A Psalm for Us* was originally meant to be a poetic diary or.. story about the things, people, and feelings i've experienced over time.. but the more i sit with it i realize it's a compilation of healing songs, healing poems, healing truth. you'll find that i've written this all in rhythm. this has become my song. my truth. and my life. i'm still learning how to become "one" with myself. i'm still learning how to stand alone. i'm still learning how to be reasonably comfortable in the thick of silence. i'm trying to find the peace amongst the voices, in my head, that often distract me. i'm trying to find myself. so hopefully.. you can learn with me.

from the seeds i've planted within, i'm finally blossoming. into everything that i'm meant to be, essentially.

i can only hope the same - for you.

xo

- *chapters* -

|

— *the blues* n. —

1. the kind of melancholy you can
only explain through song.

      recently, i made the decision to stop writing about sadness. i had a conversation with the mountains, the flowers, and the ocean. they all warned me that it was time to step away. they tried to explain how everything real dies still. each hill stood still–exemplifying freedom, acceptance, and peace. each leaf came to life, then died again, with ease. every wave made its way to the edge then returned to a familiar place. i wasn't sure if i was being taught to detach more often or if the lesson was in watching all things return back home, more frequently than i'd ever known. at times, i forget where home is.. so i build a new one just to abandon it again.

      there was an unspoken communion between everything else but me. i tried my best to take notes. kept trying to look too far into things. wouldn't let my mind keep still. couldn't just let the answers make their way to me. i watched the clouds for hours and realized the sky is in constant recovery. there's a sacred kind of compromise between, both, the moon and the sun. there's something spiritual in the way they take turns. the moon rests each day, the sun rests each night. and if you're close enough to water or mountains you can see the radiance in the reflection of their love–whenever they meet each other halfway. there is healing power amongst the silence in nature. took a while for me to welcome in balance. i spent too much time thinking and creating too many obligations for myself. i felt "heartache" was a topic i needed to place all my energy into. all along, all i really had to do was remain quiet. i kept trying to control things that are supposed to happen naturally. and so i kept failing. i kept getting sadder and sadder.. eventually, i could barely write for myself.

i glamorized the idea of helping those without a voice. i spoke about writing a book about the blues, time and time again. i wasn't aware of what i was asking god for. i knew that there was a power in the "tongue" that i could never go into great detail about—but i'd only ever experienced the positive of it. i failed to realize that the universe acts on whatever you speak into it. the only thing it knows how to do is show up when you feel love is missing. so that's why they say be careful what you ask for when you feel something's missing. first, find out what that thing is—then.. take your time deciding whether or not it's worth having again.

my intention in writing about depression was to shed light on the feeling as a whole. i wanted to be able to elaborate on what it really means to feel like there's a hole in your heart and a void in your life that you have no control over. i wanted to let people know heartbreak doesn't always have a source. sometimes the reason is unknown. i've been heartbroken almost all my life. you'd just never know because god has helped me turn my pain into something impressive. i just kept placing myself in situations to test how conditional my love could be. i just really wanted god to see. as if i were competing with someone or something else. i wanted to comfort those who felt like there was no one who could fully understand.. also, those who felt like no one could relate to what exactly they were going through. i wanted people to know that i know the feeling too. even if i never really minded being misunderstood. i never needed anyone to fully see me—i just wanted people to feel my rapture.

      someone once told me, "nothing deserves an everyday funeral." so with time i've realized we all learn in our own timing. we all let go when we're meant to. there is nothing that i can say that'll take away anyone else's gloom. there isn't anything that i can do to prevent natural disasters. there's a tsunami in your eyes that i've seen before. there's a hurricane in your voice. there's a seismic wave shaking down your spine due to the endless earthquakes.. there's a tornado in the pit of your stomach. your stomach begs to settle. your stomach can't remember the last time it was full. i know. and i promise there's a god who hears you. and i promise that a god is looking after you. i promise that something beautiful is on its way to bloom for you. i promise happiness will

find its way to you, again. i promise you'll be okay.
i promise that you'll find new love. i promise that
one day you'll be loved in return. i promise–you are
worth loving. i promise that i am someone worth
putting your trust into. we just have to have faith
through it all. we just have to hold hands through
it all. we have to believe that there will always be
light at the end of each tunnel. we have to believe in
ourselves. we have to love our entire journey. even
the tragedies. we have to let things come and pass
the way they are supposed to. we have to let go of
the past in order to elevate. to move forward. we all
have to recognize where in our lives we are the most
toxic to ourselves and find a way to plant something
infinite there.

      although i could not go further into research
for my collection of "broken" pieces.. i still need
you to know that i feel you. some days everything
is okay and others i feel like i'm dying too. for too
long i've been choking my own self to death. right
now i'm just trying to breathe. i'm just searching
for oxygen.. i'm craving peace. i'm hoping for fewer
mornings where i wonder why i'm still here. i'm
almost certain that day will come. i had to lose
everything to see how unhealthy i'd become. i had
to get down on my knees, as i was on the verge of
losing my mind, then i had to free myself.. i had to
look "me" in the mirror and create harmony with

what i could see. although, i couldn't recognize the
person i was becoming—i was willing to love
her enough to help her.

{pause.}

there's a woman i've kept to myself.
her body full of answers
her eyes full of venom
her voice haunting with resentment.
sometimes i wish i never heard her ode at all.
she's a prisoner in her own skin.
i pray for her freedom.

she always found herself in love with
the kind of people who set her heart
on fire. she couldn't resist her love,
for burning.

withdrawals

there's something ethereal about
the way she cries herself to sleep,
she holds on to nothing but her shaky skin.
her backbone is wearing out,
she can feel the sirens beneath her flesh.
she's burning from the inside out.
her stomach is a shelter for warnings.
her legs too weak to depend on.
there's wind brushing against her face,
there's vacancy in each moment.
she lies honestly in the bed she's made.
she knows bedlam better than she knows comfort—
although, she wears distress well.
her eyes heavier than heartbreak.

she sings, and sings.
she's got no faith or hope left,
just a simple melody beautiful enough
to share with god.

i've loved you with every bone in me.
every pulse. every beat.
everyone would think you've loved me back.
only sometimes. not always.
usually when i've filled you up so high;
i'm left incomplete.

still,
i search for a way..
to keep you full.

i see you

1.   there she is.
heart beating faster than brain has prepared for.
smile eager to sit straight for a while.
hands full of constant prayer.
thighs protecting a queendom.
some nights she knows her worth.

2.   there she is.
all nervous to speak up for what's hers
but will never forget what she forgot to ask for.
heart beating slower. and slower.
lips fixed. heart afraid to hear another "no."
some days she remembers
she isn't good enough.

3.   there she is.
spirit happy with the little it's got.
yet soul half empty. bones drowning in a sadness
they've failed to make a name for.
eyes full of both welcome and warning.
she's unable to let you in fast.
she's unable to let you go fast.
heart disrupted by depression, again.
heart temporarily full–again.
sometimes she's still conflicted.

4.   there she is.
attempting to remedy her damage.
still waiting on the promise of fulfillment
she was abandoned with.
lately she's been wondering what it takes.
heart working on becoming
anything other than the prey.
she'll come over here someday
she'll meet me here - some way.
dying to learn my ways.
craving to love me better.
but only after she's found her place
within this bodysuit.

not today

i was told all poems have titles.
this is how they're remembered.
someone gets lucky enough to name them
then send 'em off into the world.
to me, this sounds like attachment.
and i cannot bear to love anything
that will leave me, someday.
not today, at least.

come apart

i talk to myself with the same words i wish to speak
to past lovers;
in i've seen better days,
in gloom.
in optimism.
in doubt. in uncertainty.
in assurance.
in "i'm pretty sure.."
in "it always gets better"
in "i hate yous."
in "i like yous."
in confusion.
i long for a deeper kind of worship.
i want to be recognized as something exceptional.
i want to know what love feels like.
i want to know if, this—was love.
i want to hear its voice.
i want to sing her song to you.
i want you to listen.
i wish shit were different.
i don't understand this.
sometimes, things were good,
sometimes, things were bad.
things could be better, i guess.

fruitless

i'm constantly searching for the mother in me.
i'm searching for the rebirth, the pain, the beauty.
searching for the selflessness
to give life to a bed of seeds.
wondering when or how or if i'll ever be ready.
as if my damaged mother was, at sixteen.
or her drug-addicted mother, at fourteen.
or her immigrant mother, at thirteen.
i wonder if the fearlessness skipped me.
i wonder if being a mother just isn't meant for me.
or if i've become so detached to what's real
and distracted by what's temporary.
this ego.
this vain.
this promise to myself it'll happen
when it's meant to be.
this belief that in order to give life
you have to be "ready."
as if we've taken courses on "the right time."
when is the "right time"?
will you show me?
will you help me understand?
will you listen?
will you promise not to judge me?
will you accept me despite my flaws?

i'm constantly searching for forever.
as if i've known it before.
as if i was familiar with it.
i'm searching for someone to offer me comfort.
i'm searching for a person who feels like safety.
but there goes that arrogance again.
that fear of the unknowing.
that belief that i have a say—
on when, or where, or how
i plant life.

storytelling

recently i met a women who wanted to tell me her
truths. she thought i was trustworthy enough to
keep them to myself. i warned her that she was
wrong about me. i asked her twice if she was sure.
with the little to no emotion she had left inside,
she insisted i listen.
she said, "it's hard to be honest with people
who think that they know you well."
"so listen to my story from an outside perspective.
and please, try not to judge me.
or.. maybe that's what i need. someone else's
opinion on why i can't get this shit right.
and.. why i can't seem to understand that
i have to love me better.
in order for someone else to ever truly love me,
i need to love me first. right?
because the truth is—
i'm constantly bleeding.
i'm constantly needing to love somebody.
i'm constantly needing to be loved.
maybe i really just need somebody's confirmation.
maybe i don't believe in myself enough
to trust my gut feeling.
maybe i need you to tell me that i'm sorry.
maybe i need you to remind me that i'm worthy.

maybe i need to hear it from someone else.
maybe i just don't trust me anymore.
maybe i've made too many bad decisions.
shouldn't have held on too tight.
shouldn't have waited.
shouldn't have forgotten
that eve was made for adam
so now woman is all man got.
shouldn't have forgotten that she was made
for him because man was made lonely
and he searches for her when he needs saving.
because only woman provides healing.
and only women provide heaven.
provide security. provide comfort. provide life.
maybe it isn't me who needs to be
healed or held tight.
maybe i misunderstood.
maybe i was told i was worthless.
maybe i've been searching for importance ever
since. or meaning; or reason.. to love me better.
maybe i've spent so much time bettering others
i forgot nothing about me is broken.
or unworthy.
just tired. just bruised. just restoring,
for the next person
who will listen..
to my story."

no apologies

lately, when i'm asked "how are you?"
i tell the truth.
i look people so far into their eyes,
i know they feel the ground shake.
i'm certain they regret breaking silence
once my voice sings,
"exhausted out my mind
scared for my life, counting my days -
today might be my last."
there's a certain kind of gospel that shouts
"hallelujah!"
this isn't one of them.
i'm tired of making comfortable beds
that i will never get to lie in.
i'm sick of catering to people
whom i will never get to lie with - forever.
i kiss my loved ones goodbye
every time we part ways
just in case
we have to meet in another life.

see, i know i'm close to the ending.
here, in this country that's set me free
i've been robbed of my glory.
here, in this country that's promised me peace
i've been abused, misled, and raped
all by men who swore they'd love me.
here, on this land where
my great-grandmother prays for me
i've had to question if there
was a god who cared for me.
i've had to question if god
was something more real than a daydream.
do you know what it's like
to go to sleep at night
wishing this
was the ending?

memorial

you may have forgotten me by now,
but here's the truth.
i hate to watch you smile from a distance.
we never hung out much but i still find myself
reminiscing
about the moment we met and how, instantly,
we connected.
my hurt will never not mention you.
my best poems are still full of gloom
my hands.. never too full for you,
if ever you wonder.
my heart. still empty.
my mind knows better.
so instead of writing you,
i'll leave it here.
whenever i get high i still think of you.
i think about the way you laugh.
i think about the way you sing.
i think about all those nights we lay together,
no kissing, no touching.
just vibes. just energy.
the truth is,
i wish you cared more about my well-being.
the truth is,
i wish i knew more about yours.

why don't you act like you know me enough?
how did you forget the way i love?
since when do i have to remind you who this is?
you don't remember me?
you don't remember my heart?
you don't remember falling apart
every time i'd leave?
you don't remember the artsy things?
like a love after a love after a love
worth writing about?
you don't remember our song?
you don't remember writing it?
you don't remember singing to me?
remember saying you missed me?
remember needing to speak to me?
to hear from me?
remember me?
remember us?
remember..
anything?

i've fought my way into hearts,
i've fought just to keep them.
although, i've never fought my way out -
i often find myself fighting for lovers
who would never fight to keep me.

the truth:

sometimes i'm not okay. and that's okay.
i'm exhausted. there's nothing wrong with that.
i'm tired of giving away my heart constantly
and receiving things in return that are conditional.
i'm tired of being a victim.
i want to be loved the same in return.
every day is a process for me.
i'm trying to be more understanding.
i'm trying to be more open to the reality that
not everyone is going to need me back.
and i'm trying to be okay with that.
it's nothing personal.
some people just don't know any better.
some people just don't even know
what it means to love with no boundaries.
with no limitations. with no expectations.
with no requirements.
every day i wonder.. do i require too much?
do i expect too much?

sweet, sexy

silly of me to think you'd remember me.
like, i don't give the time of day to people who don't
really even know me.
like, i ain't used to being the kind of lover who
receives a love that's conditional.
i can't blame you for leaving.
or, for thinking i was a certain kind of woman.
or for thinking i wasn't the kind of chick
you could bring home to
your mother who's probably more
like me than you know.
more than likely, she's been a victim too.
of not being able to be a freak
and make good pancakes too.
of not being able to be sweet and sexy too.
i'm sure she taught you better than that.
you must have forgotten how i stripped for you.
how i let you see my heart regardless of the scars
and how i still held you by the hand when you
realized you were falling for a woman who's been
forced to have the mindset of
a savage.

trauma

i can still remember the way you felt.
the chaos in each touch.
there was war in your fingertips,
a battle on your tongue.
blood filled my lungs.

i was helpless.

i wish i would have known a way to simply imply,
"stop."
i must have assumed you'd look up at me.
i wish your body could feel my mourning.
i wish you could taste my grief.
i wasn't whole enough to fight.
you made me.
although,
sometimes i know it was my fault.
maybe i shouldn't have been so curious
or in a rush to experience
true love.

this might have been avoided,
if i was shown
true love.

i wish we really loved each other,
to know each other better.

maybe you would have known
i don't like to be touched.
or i really don't even like the idea of us
pretending.
to be something we are not.
to be
man and woman,
emotional and heavy,
unconditional; and ready.
i don't remember ever being ready.
i don't ever even remember saying "yes."
you decided for me.
you thought we made sense
together.
i can't bear to remember you.
disturbed of our memories.

trauma was the name your mother gave you.

is this me?

there's a weight on my shoulder that i can't seem to
shake.. there are chills down my spine that sting me
till exhaustion. i can't feel my heart beat.. i'm trying
to be okay. there's a brick on my chest every time i
breathe in—then out. i cough at the thought of
freedom, or peace of mind.

right now things don't feel good.
though, i can feel more right now than usual.
i can feel myself disappearing to this person.
this castaway. this disappointment.
i can barely differentiate whose shadow is whose.

the loneliest loneliness

your silence always reminds me why on my loneliest
nights i run toward pain.

things you've said before

wish you were here.

                                                    wish you loved me.

wish you truly understood.

                                                    wish you remembered.

wish you held on.

                                                    wish you forgot
about our differences.

                                                    wish you warned me.

wish you spared me.

                                                wish you cared to say sorry.

i'm sorry..

                                                    i just, miss you.

i don't want to live a life without you.

                                                    i don't want to fall in love again.

i don't want—to miss you.

                                                    i don't want to search for better..

i don't want to forget

                                                    about our differences.

i don't want to own up to it.

i think you're overreacting.

i think it's worth another shot.

i can help you change your mind.

wish you were near

to talk.

to hear me out.

to see my heart.

to love me.

to remind you

what you mean to me.

i know you must have loved me.

you held me hard—by choice.

like you meant it.

like you wanted to.

like, you needed to.

please.   i need you, too.

tell your mother i apologize.
tell her i'm sorry we ever crossed paths
or tell her the truth is, i'm sorry i found you.
i noticed the door was unlocked
so i helped myself in.
you were more than simply beautiful.
i was stunned by the majestic view.
tell her i never meant to intrude,
i tried to be silent.
tell her i'm sorry she disapproved.
there were no beware signs
and there was no alarm.
i strayed your way
while i was wandering.
i felt your spirit from a mile away.
i could hear the angels chatter on your shoulders.
tell your mother i meant no harm.
tell her i only wanted to protect you.
and tell her i'm sorry
i wasn't the person she wanted for you.

reasons i'm often sad

1. i let people take advantage of me too often. i
    don't know how to say no without feeling guilty.
    apologies and proposals and love songs are never
    as sincere as they used to be. but still, i'm sorry
    if i've ever made you feel i don't need you. i do,
    more than you know. this layer of my heart is
    still waiting to shed. recently i've been learning
    more about myself, and i realized i became far
    too attached to memories, and i always catch
    myself thinking about shit like—growing old with
    people who are no longer in my life.

2. my father calls me less often these days. i guess
    he realized it's rare that i pick up. but i hope he
    knows i wish i could talk to him about how i
    wish things were different and i wish we could
    go back to old times and i wish we could share
    our fears again. i wish i had the courage to speak
    the truth to him.

3. vegan options are, still, not as common as you'd
    think. i know how it feels to be hungry for
    something life isn't offering. i'm used to starving
    myself, or wanting more than, both people and
    places are willing to offer me. or more than i can
    afford if they ever decided to. and i know the
    feeling of not being thought of, all too well.

4. there isn't enough greenery in the city.

5. the traffic in los angeles is getting worse, day by day. it's starting to take me over an hour to get to almost any destination.. and in this hour, i've got time to think about why i should have stayed in and why i should never leave the house and why i fit better alone anyway. i also have time to think about life; and when i start to think about my life i start to realize that i've always been a compilation of the blues. and whether i'm in love with the story or not, i don't think i have a choice but to offer my soul to it. i have to gather these songs and hum every note and pray that there's someone listening.. i don't know if this is a classic and i don't know if i've broken the curse yet.. i just know that it's all true. everything i seem to be. everything you think of me. this is what it means to believe in the moon. i'm okay with however you perceive me. i've been on autopilot for quite some time—so i can barely recollect how i've ended up here. and so i've decided it probably isn't very safe to sit still for too long and have to think about life or anything at all. over time, i've developed an anxiety to almost everything that requires my energy. and traffic. well traffic requires the kind of energy that i don't have lately.

6. i remember the first time i had ever felt like a woman. i was getting eye fucked and loud shouts

from men i was never curious to know. i grew hips big enough for a bystander to notice, as if my latina genes were finally kicking in and it was time for me to grow into myself. my celestial body was starting to celebrate itself. my hesitant lips were plumping, my cheekbones were creating a name for themselves, and my hair was getting more obnoxious by the second. from time to time my mom would go out of her way to tell me, "being hairy is beautiful." but, despite her efforts, i don't know what it's like to feel beautiful.. i was never familiar with the feeling of being watched or being wanted, so i never learned how to hide in convenience.

7. my brown skin is up for auction without my consent.

8. these feelings no longer mean much. although, i learned how to keep them to myself, years ago. this silence is golden—it has protected me from getting in trouble or sold, even. although, it hasn't kept me from shattering. there are pieces of me lying everywhere; i haven't been able to join them together, i think i am lost.

9. for years i kept needing to be held, i've had nowhere to go, there hasn't been a person who has loved me for the deeper things.

10. recently i found myself in hiding. i'm still afraid to come out.

11. this afternoon i was searching the internet for good interviews and writing inspiration. and i stumbled upon a high school poetry grand slam. usually i wouldn't have been interested but for a split second i was in awe. i thought to myself, "i wish i could remember what this felt like." palms sticky with perspiration, hands shaking feverishly, voice cracking at every loss of breath. i miss loving something so deeply i'm willing to dedicate my all to it, regardless of fear. i miss writing without having to smoke trees. i miss feeling free. i miss what it felt like to know myself enough to write from within. i miss–feeling.

limerence

i may be too late but i've been meaning to tell you,
you've always been my favorite poem.
you've always spoke volumes,
even in the depths of silence.
sometimes, i crave your silence.
i can taste the sirens in your tongue.
i can hear the softness in your heart.
i can see you for what you're truly worth.
was it worth it? to lose me?
to fight your way into another heart?
to give up everything we've worked so hard for?
to walk away from a situation
that had so much potential?
to forget why we started "this"?
the excuses have been endless.
i don't mind not hearing anything.
i don't mind finding the truth within the fiction.
i still admire your silence.
i just don't care to believe you weren't man enough.
i just don't think you tried hard enough.
i just don't think you understood this kind of love.
despite your ways or despite our differences,
i just wanted to show you something real.

sometimes, i still do.

chance

there's a saying about folding
and how it's never right to do.
but sometimes i'll bend
just to be right for you.
maybe, i'm a fool.
but maybe.. just maybe..
you're a fool for me too.

weary heart

because of you i'm terrified of people.
i avoid conversation in passing
because i'm afraid i'm always
the only one who holds on.
i don't want to let them in,
i don't want to let you go.
i haven't had a chance to stop remembering.
i haven't found a way to withdraw myself yet.
i don't want to be left behind again.
i don't want to fall in love again.
because of you—love is my only weakness.
the only reason i stay up late at night,
thinking of everything i shouldn't.
wondering, why
we couldn't make this right.
wondering, how
you thought this was best for us.
as if you didn't already know,
i thought you were best for me.
you must have loved me at some point.
we mustn't forget the truth.
you vowed to never stop trying.
how could you forget our roots?
we planted to always be together.
was the weather that bad?

when did you learn i wasn't worth it?
are you happy with your new location?
i want to hear your lies, again.
i can find the prayer in them.
give me something to believe in.
give me pain to grow from and forget.
give me hope.
i'm not afraid to get
my heart broken by you.
i know the feeling..
only this time
i'll be prepared.
i'll volunteer.
i'll tell myself it's okay,
to love again.

like you and me

somehow.. i always end up in places that i was never
meant to be.. with people like you who would watch
while i bleed. i could pour out my heart until i can't
feel it beating and you wouldn't hesitate to ask why
you can still feel me breathing.
i end up in places, wrapped around in lust, and
humility—carrying your satisfaction along with the
guilt that lives within me. i carry you in places,
where i never prepared myself to be..
wondering why love has become so difficult to see.
wondering why i can't see that love and lust are two
separate things. wondering if companionship is even
realistic for someone like me. questioning where
along the lines you became a part of me.
somehow.. i always end up with you in mind.
wondering if people like you are a reflection of me,
or if i got so used to being left i began to carry you
all with me. holding on to things that were never
meant for me has always been
a part of my tendencies.
lately, i've ended up in places, where love has
become more and more frightening. places i'm all
too unfamiliar with. places with people who would
bleed for me. pouring out their heart until i can see
i'm the reason it's beating.

places people like you would never dare bring me.
somehow.. i always find myself in places -
dreaming, that it was really you
who wanted me, too.

but people like you.. never really do.

apologies

mother,
i am sorry if i've ever let you down.
or if, i've ever ended up with the men you so
desperately tried to warn me of.
i am sorry if i've ever held on too tight.
or if, i ever let go of the person who was right for
me. i know how much you'd like to see me happy.
i am sorry if i've ever broken your heart.
and if, i've ever held back my tongue during
conversations you couldn't wait to have.
i apologize for sharing my art with the world before
you. i am sorry if i've ever disappointed you.
and if, you've ever found out about the lies i swore
were true. and if, you've ever had to wonder if i
were still your daughter. the one you tried so hard to
raise to be just like you.
loving.. kind.. and strong.
i know there were days
where i proved i wasn't..
loving, kind, or strong.

father,
i am sorry if i've ever let you down.
if, i've ever ended up with men like yourself.
men who i thought were my superman
or my hero. i'm sorry if i'm offending you.
i'm sorry if your prayers for me never made it
through. i am sorry if i've ever made love to
someone who wasn't right for me. i am sorry if i've
ever made love to someone who wouldn't fight for
me. i'm sorry for never giving you the credit you
deserve. i know how hard you worked to make sure i
was protected from the world. men, specifically.
you loved me enough to scare the boys away,
but now the boys have gotten older
and they haven't a fear in the world.
they've come nearer, they've come closer.
they've broken my heart. over and over.
my mom always says they remind her of you.
i'm sorry this is how she remembers you.

now or later on

sometimes i feel like i can be toxic to the people
around me. i harbor so many ill, shitty feelings
inside, and eventually i just pour them all onto
everyone and everything surrounding me.
of course i don't mean to.. but sometimes i have no
control over it. or.. control over myself i guess i
should say. i try to be—and stay—as positive as
humanly possible, but god.. i'm so tired. i'm tired of
never having an outlet. i'm tired of being
everyone else's outlet and not being thought of in
return. i don't mean to be sad all the time but i
genuinely can't even help it. i could probably get
better at attacking problems and situations as they
present themselves so that i don't always do these
massive blowup things. but.. i haven't reached that
point of detachment just yet. i'm still working on
me. i'm still a project in progress. hopefully, i get
better at being a better person. soon.
or someday.

the things that haunt me:

1. for one year now i've been conflicted with
    whether now is the time to announce i have a
    disease, or.. if i should keep up this act that i've
    got it all together. it seems to get me by. it seems
    to make others believe that i'm never in need
    of being checked up on. a couple months back
    i diagnosed myself as empty. i have a kind of
    sadness that cannot be named or explained to
    the happy folk. i have the kind of bruise that
    never lightens and consecutive bad days that only
    heighten. every day i'm in need of something
    stronger. something stronger than weed. someone
    stronger than me. something or someone godly
    enough to save me.

2. for two years i've been conflicted with whether
    my mother finally had enough or if she simply
    gave up. maybe she was tired of holding on to the
    lies my father fed her and decided she wanted a
    better meal. maybe she was too weak to carry the
    weight he placed on her back when he repeatedly
    said, "i don't love you enough to change." i can
    still hear her preach about how when love is real
    you gather your bones and make supper anyway.
    you neglect the aches and keep on - day after
    day after day. you place a lock on every closet so

skeletons won't find a way to reveal themselves
when things seem to be going "okay." every now
and again i can see her and my father laughing
on our living room sofa. every now and again i
can see her by her lonesome crying on our front
porch. every now and again i wonder if i was
the result of a holy woman praying for a man to
change. every now and again i wish i were reason
enough for my father's change.

3. for three years i've been conflicted with whether
    there is any truth in the words my ex spoke about
    me practically being a waste of an investment, or
    if he was a part of the majority who could see my
    magic and inevitably - tried to steal my power
    away. i wouldn't be surprised if he became afraid
    of the love i gave. he might have been afraid to
    see me in my final form. i might have mistaken
    him to be the honest kind of people. or, i might
    just really not be magic at all. i might just really
    not be the kind of person you'd want to love. i
    wouldn't doubt myself to be an illusion. truthfully,
    i doubt i'm the kind of person you don't fully
    see. truthfully, he might have mistaken me to be
    worthy before truly knowing me. truthfully, i'm
    still trying to deem my own self worthy.

4. for four years i've been conflicted with the idea
    that someday soon i'll have a baby. i'll give birth
    to a half full moon because deficiencies run in

my DNA. every single day i wonder if today is the day god promised me. the one where i was reassured that someday i won't have to worry. every day i wonder if god was lying to me the same way the men promised to stay while they lied right beside me. i'm still praying that one day i'll, at the very least, be left half full and not left half ruined. the women in my family might agree that somewhere along the line we were cursed.. i wish i were proof enough to disagree with that. i've been conflicted because some days i decide i shouldn't. i decide that maybe it's best i save the world by being the last of a dying breed and showing the world that miracles are real because my mother birthing me made her lucky. every day she still thanks me.

5. for five years i've been trying to figure out the definition of my dreams and why they always seem to come to fruition. at 17 i began dreaming that i wouldn't live past 24. however, i'm conflicted because at 22 i don't feel very alive anymore. in fact, i don't feel anything at all anymore. i'm just allowing life to come and pass as i wait for two years. i'm just allowing love to come and pass as i wait for my dreams to come to fruition.

6. for six years now, i've been wondering. i've been thinking about that night on christmas eve—the time i met all five of my brothers and sisters. the

moment my youngest sister shouted "daddy" to
a man, so familiar, i thought i knew. to the same
man i called daddy, too. to a being who was once
my superhero. wasn't sure if i was trippin' or if the
lady holding her hand was her mother. or if the
lady holding her hand was once my babysitter.
wasn't sure if it was all real. some things you
forget—this i couldn't. i mean.. shorty took me
to see *The Lion King.* wasn't aware then that my
father was the lying king. i was told there were
only two. i was told of Arianna and JuJu. but
forreal though.. for six years i've been keeping this
a secret. conflicted. with whether or not i should
tell my mother. i know for sure she was never
warned about Jeffrey, Jacob, and Mia, too. i just
know how fragile she can be. i know every time
she hears something ugly about a man she could
only ever find beauty in—her heart shatters by the
dozens. i know i've prayed to clear my conscience.
i know i've asked god to fill the spaces where
truth doesn't. or where comfort hasn't. i know
she's going to see them one day. i know i could
probably prepare her. i know, i'm probably no
better than my father. i just don't know right from
wrong here.

7. for seven years i've been conflicted with the
    reality of whether it was my fault or it was my
    "god" who decided a man's touch was what was

best for me. i remember being curious but i'm
not positive i was willing to see what it truly
felt like. i remember feeling the tension in the
room simply after i refused, but i'm not positive
he heard me. although, i must have heard my
daddy's voice, as he touched my thigh, saying
"girl, you know better than that." and i must have
heard my mama's voice, as he gripped the back of
my head saying, "why must you always learn the
hard way?" i'm not positive i was ready for the
answer in the storm, or the thunder, or the quakes
after each night it rained or after each night i
prayed myself to sleep. i walked around for two
weeks trying to replay how it went and if anyone
could see the filth amongst me. i walked around
for two years looking for someone who could
genuinely make love to me. i walked around in
hopes finding someone who could see that i was
much more than just a set of voluptuous hips and
an elastic spine that would look expensive in a
u-shaped position.

8. took me eight years after i thought i knew love to
   actually find love. real love. that set you free. that
   healthy love. or so i think. i'm still conflicted.

abusive
addictions

addiction is continuously running back to a person, place, or vice that makes you feel really good— sometimes. addiction is knowing when things have played their part in our lives, but being unable to let go, even after we've recognized they have already served their purpose. abuse can be an addiction.

- epiphany -

this time last year i was completely broken. i lost a love that i thought was endless. i watched the person i thought was meant for me, move on to love someone new. i had no one to talk to. i had no one to turn to. too many people telling me to get over it, and not enough people trying to be understanding of the position i was in. everyone thought i was as strong as i thought i was; or as strong as i thought i used to be. i became more and more of an introvert. i stayed to myself. i battled my own thoughts. i let nothing out. i was working a job that made me miserable. i was in school, trying to figure it out.. trying to figure out what i wanted for my life. my parents were going through a breakup that i probably should have been ready or prepared for.. but the timing was off. my heart wasn't ready for any form of destruction or abandonment. and not too long after, my best friend decided to move to australia. i was lost. and i had no idea what i wanted.. i had no ambition to do anything more than the bare minimum.. even if i could figure out what i wanted to do with my life—i was weak.

throughout the course of my life, i have spent an abundance of time helping others. i've listened, i've accepted, and i've helped guide whomever i could. i spent so much time trying to fix people—i would have never considered myself insufficient. i never wanted to be a burden on anyone, even if, i never

felt others were a burden to me. i never thought
a person's energy could be in jeopardy. i never
figured that person would be me, either. i never paid
close enough attention to the way my voice shook
whenever i was internally depleted. i just kept going.
i could never find myself giving up on people who
i felt had already given up on themselves. and so i
never put myself before or in front of anyone. i never
felt i had to.

      what i remember the most, was one night,
i got stoned and rushed into the shower. i had no
strength to stand up so i fell onto the floor of my tub
and couldn't help but to cry my heart out. i felt like
my life had fallen apart and there were no signs to
prepare me. i kept shouting "why god? why me?"
i considered myself a victim. i felt like i was being
played with or punished and i had no reasoning as
to why. soon after i broke down, i became angry.
i became so furious and frustrated that, almost
immediately, i could feel my life changed. after a
half hour's worth of tears, i completely shut down
and had an out-of-body experience. i looked at
myself, from the outside in and said, "what the hell
are you even really crying for? i know you know
better. i know you have more strength than this."
followed with, "you thought this would be easy?"
and in that moment everything changed.

i got out of the shower, looked myself in
the mirror and prayed. my entire tone shifted from
"god, why are you doing this to me?" to "god, i
think i get it now." "i may not know.. and i may not
see the reasoning behind everything, but i'm trusting
you with me. i'm giving myself to you for recovery."
and i stuck alongside my word. that night i washed
away all the sorrow, all the pity, all the doubt, and
all the fear every bone in me could carry. that night
i won the biggest battle ever thrown at me. and i
kept on. day by day i got stronger. i forced myself to
become tenacious and wiser. i kept busy at all hours
trying to do almost anything i could to keep from
allowing myself to wander back to that broken state
of mind. i read book after book. i fell in love with a
countless amount of characters. i hiked mountain
after mountain, ran mile after mile.. i fell in love
with nature. i also fell in love with my physical
appearance. then.. i set goals. i became hungry.
hungry for change. hungry for growth. hungry for
fulfillment. i became eager to feel love from within.
i wanted nothing more than to love my own self,
deeper than anyone else could ever love me.. in
addition to.. more than i could ever love anyone else,
in return.

soon after—i began searching for myself;
then i started writing. in the process, and in the
midst of everything, i became so lost in my journey

that heartbreak was so far in the past i forgot
what heartache felt like. i forgot what it felt like
to feel anyone or anything deeply. then one night
i remembered. that night i turned to god for the
millionth time and asked, "why me?" supposing that
i was in a different state of mind than when i usually
inquire–the deepest chills ran through my body.
although it took months for me to conceive any
kind of explanation, when i did.. i was ready. and
i was open to take it all in, and i was willing to be
as understanding as possible. the answers presented
themselves in powerful segments. "why me?" well..
because i have the power of tongue. i have the
power of vulnerability. i have the power to act so
transparently that people forget i'm human too. more
often than not, others forget i'm normal, too.

      i used to hate the idea of love. i grew up
watching love done wrong for so long that i started
to believe it was a place or a thing or a feeling
that i didn't want any parts of. i watched love
backfire in the faces of all of my loved ones.. so i
stopped believing in marriage and all things that
were permanent. when i was younger i purposely
involved myself with people just to hurt them. my
method of protecting my own heart was to not truly
use it but to make people think that i did. and so
eventually.. i harmed myself. i began losing people
and things that really meant a great deal to me. even

though, initially, i was unaware of their impact on
me. i started catching feelings for those who were
no good. my father taught me that you are who
you attract. so, inevitably, i started falling in love
with people who were just like me. they'd hurt me,
misuse and mistreat me. they'd show me the side of
myself that i was never used to. still, i'm so relieved
i saw her when i did and i'm so thankful that i felt
hurt about it. sadly, i couldn't make out who i had
turned into. it wasn't until i truly fell apart that i
realized how much it took to rebuild back into who
i was or who i was meant to be. because really.. i
was never meant to be heartless.. i never meant to
tear people apart. i'm a lover. i always have been.
it took me some time to be comfortable with my
truth, but nowadays i love that about me. i love
that i've become more aware of how important it is
that i do whatever i can to protect as many hearts
as i can, even if that means to love and take care of
them myself. even if that means to love them from a
distance. i love that there are people who respect and
trust me enough to pour all of their love into me.
unconditional love is what has set me free.

  finally, i learned the most suitable answer to
the question "why me?" that i had been asking for
years. "me"—because i've lived my life constantly
asking god to "use" me. i've prayed to god, time
and time again, asking for guidance. i spoke these

words before knowing the true power in our tongue. i asked god for a purpose, and i asked that in fulfilling that purpose, i'm able to continue growing. sometimes growth comes with mishaps. so going through adversity and discomfort is inevitable. but here i am. one year later. in love. with a person who i mean everything to. happier than i've ever been. mentally stable. spiritually balanced. emotionally ready and open;

for any- and everything.

{breathe.}

i have already lost touch with the person i used to
be—so please do not come looking for her.

she has left. she has been lost. she has been found.
she has changed. she's different.
for better, or worse, it is too early to tell.

she has learned from her mistakes. she has put her
foot down. she doesn't play games or like to bullshit.
she don't hang around much. she's hardly accessible.
she has developed.

she has a fruitful kind of energy. she protects herself
now. she has bloomed. she has expanded her mind.

she has known earthquake longer than she has
known the calm. she guards her heart much more
than then. she knows better. sometimes, i reminisce
about
the person she used to be but she's grown into
someone i'm more than happy to be.

someone who's happier.

i've never not been a poem;
imperfect but beautiful as fuck.

what i'm discovering
about myself:

1. i'd rather be in my head and left alone.
2. capitalizing on the things you love is a wicked game. lately i've been losing. lately i've been empty. not broken or hurt or confused; just empty. still, i give my all. i search within for whatever's left. whatever hurt, whatever feelings, whatever love. i don't give up even when i have nothing left to give.
3. i've officially outgrown my past. i've finally let go. i'm finally moving on. i no longer resent my father. i no longer ignore my mother. i no longer search for dysfunction in lovers.
4. my energy is my most valuable possession. physical, mental, emotional, and spiritual. so valuable—i'm afraid to jeopardize it. i'm too afraid to lose all that i've worked so hard to become. recently, i've been trusting fear more than i trust myself.
5. really good music is my preference. over anything. over everything. i'd rather spend my time searching for something beautiful than to settle for what's given to me.

6. i should probably be more receiving and/or
   accepting of the things that are given to me.
   i've never been good at balance. although.. i'm
   working on it. i promise myself this.

7. i used to write as therapy. now i seek therapy
   when i'm unable to write. maybe i've abused my
   powers. maybe they were never powers to begin
   with. i think i think too much.

8. i'm always conflicted these days. i don't
   remember the last time i had a strong opinion.
   on anything. and i'm kind of okay with that.
   maybe i sympathize with both sides of the story.
   i don't know. i'm perplexed.

what other women might say

woman,
you forgot your coconut oil
and your jewelry
and your mascara
and your pink polish
and your red lipstick
and your smile that could comfort anyone.
you forgot—to wax your upper lip
and your armpits
and your voice when spoken to
and your silence when not.
you forgot to iron your blouse
and to sit up straighter than everyone else.
you forgot your corset
you forgot your favorite fragrance
you forgot to hold your breath
you forgot to please them.
don't worry, there will be another chance soon.
there will be another boy,
another man, another people—
to come and judge you someday,
make sure you're ready.

make sure you're prepared to play the game,
prepared to stick up for yourself,
prepared to act holy,
prepared to show,
you were built for this.
even though—the truth is
you aren't the kind to "put up with shit."
there's only really one kind of you
from my experience.
only one type of woman
decent enough
for men.
find a way
to become her.

if you aren't,
already.

softer

i'm trying my best to be softer these days.
i overheard someone say, "it must be so difficult to
find love when the way you love just seems to be so
terrifying."
i never meant to present my heart this way.. never
meant for anyone to confuse falling in love with
going insane. i never meant to love too hard. i never
meant to scare anyone away. i'm learning to be okay
when people go astray.
i overheard someone say, "not everyone is meant for
you and that's why not everyone can stay."
i never meant to chase and chase. i never meant to
treat people like my prey. i never meant to hunt for
the person's heart that fulfilled me most. i never
meant to impose myself. i never meant to force my
hunger for something real upon anyone. i never
meant to be a burden. i'm trying my best to be more
understanding of "fate." i never meant to love too
hard. i never meant to scare anyone away.

> i'm trying my best
> to be softer somehow..
> someway.

before putting forth blame,
acknowledge that abuse doesn't always come from
an outside source.
sometimes we abuse ourselves.
mentally, emotionally, physically, spiritually.

|

free yourself.

i'm one of "those."
one of the ones who "hurt" too hard.
one of the ones who've been loved too soft.
i'm one of those lovers who gives so much "me" away,
that i'm left with nothing at all.
not clarity. not an apology. not a proper withdraw.
not a forever. not love. not a promise left whole.
not a "maybe one day" or a "maybe never at all"
not an explanation. not an excuse.
not a warning sign and certainly, not the truth.

i'm one of "those."
one of the ones who thinks too much.
one of the ones who talks too little.
one of the ones who "doesn't speak up" quite often;
or.. who comes off "too strong" if ever i'd decided
to. i'm one of the ones whose "heart" can't take it.
whose poem wasn't enough to keep anyone around.
whose song was left incomplete because the words
weren't really that great, after all..
i'm one of those—who has only ever been the
chorus. one of the ones who is appealing but never
not interchangeable. one of the ones who's only
ever compared.. or forgotten.
i'm one of the ones who sees it all,
but who always leaves it alone.

i'm one of "those."
one of the ones who's only ever been a hindrance.
who's never been hard to leave.
who's never not left incomplete.
one of those who'd rather complete someone else.
who never thinks of self, first.
i'm one of the ones who's always had to compete,
for a love that never fully belonged to me.
i'm one of the ones who.. just keeps on.
who just keeps trying
to be loved,
in return.

my goal has always been to be
so unconditionally loving
that it fills the hearts of others
who are empty from a lack of.

for those who think
they know me:

1. this wasn't meant to rub you wrong in any kind
    of way.. or to make you question me. i just felt
    you should know, truthfully you don't know
    me like you think you do. and i don't mean to
    be rude or to make you any kind of confused
    but sometimes your ideas of me make me
    uncomfortable. you see, the real me may not
    be who you care for. that's why we truly don't
    speak often and we see each other almost never.
    i wish there was no obligation or requirement
    to be your friend. like staying this person you
    think i might be or coming around when you
    need me most. the truth is sometimes i won't
    make it. and the truth is sometimes i might not
    even try. and the truth is sometimes i might just
    lie. and the truth is sometimes i may just not feel
    fine. i'm realizing i've played pretend for so long
    just for the sake of keeping a friend. for having
    someone to call, sometimes. for being someone
    to call, sometimes. some nights i lie up and think
    too much. some nights i prefer that. i prefer to
    stay home and stick to myself and usually i don't
    know why that is. i just know that you don't

really even know me. the real me. and i know
that for sure because i'm fairly sure - i don't even
truly know myself.

2. i'm all the bad men my mother warned me
   about. i'm every broken being i was told to stay
   away from.. i'm all good until nobody's looking.
   to everyone i'm all but aching because i've
   learned.. things are much more beautiful this
   way. things are easier this way.

3. i'm not really a poet. i just make simple words
   sound good.

4. i have no fight left in me. ain't got no strength
   to move along. ain't got no real love for the real
   me. don't know what it's like to be taken care
   of. sometimes that bothers me.. but sometimes,
   i prefer to keep me to myself. i don't mind being
   alone.

because i spoke you into existence,
i believe we were meant to create something much
richer than the word "beautiful" implies.
something *holy.*

because i've been watching you love and ache, from
a distance, my heart sings for you.
i'll be here with the *blues* if you need me.

i've got jazz too, for the cleansing..
because you've bled yourself to sleep and arose
by morning, a thousand times,
i've never seen someone so godly.
someone so *magic.*
do you know what it's like to wait for you?
because i've been watching you *build and break* from a
distance, my arms will welcome your body closer.
but i will not beg or plead or influence.

because of art you will forever be a part in my story.
because i've watched you mend—again and again,
i want you to see how inspiring you are.
to be a *woman* unafraid to love
a woman who loves herself.

my worry will never lie with you.
only *refuge.* only *prayer.* only *worship.*

ansisters

i know they must've mentioned my name.
they must have thought of my existence.
must have spoke it to the stars. must have prayed.
i know the odds are too unlikely.
i know having skin too dark and hair too nappy.
i know oppress, digress, and silence.
i know rejection better than i know my own name.
still, i hide behind silence.
i kept thinking someone must have lied
when they called me queen, but maybe..
maybe there was hope.
maybe they noticed freedom before it came.
maybe my ancestors still root for me.
maybe the seeds are planted deeper than i'll ever
see. maybe i'm overthinking.
maybe this was destiny.
maybe i was designed to prevail and influence.
maybe we all were.
i've heard plenty of times that god shows up tardy
in the midst of bedlam.
but maybe *she* was right on time.
i know they must have seen her before.
i know she made a promise.
maybe i was that promise.
maybe, she promised to show up for me.

aren't we so forgetful?

love is love is love.
we all want it. we all need it.
we all search for it in others.
we all forget to search in ourselves.

self-love

the first time i fell in love with a woman,
i was paying far too close attention to the way her
lips moved. i watched her words form into a body of
fluid. she spoke so eloquently. i regret not knowing
how beautiful she'd be or i might have prepared
myself to fall. or maybe i'd forgotten how the moon
shines. actually, i forgot that stars are constantly
aligning. and how us women are designed to be love.
she was nothing less than. although, just "love"
might be too dull a description for the way i felt
about her spirit. she spoke from her soul
and demanded me to listen. then asked, if i fully
understood. she said "love's too big a miracle to
assume anything, less than likely. or to think you
have control, speaking of preference." "you think
you fall in love with people that you choose?" she
wondered. "i can promise you, you didn't choose
me." she didn't need to do any convincing, in order
for me to believe it. i was confident, i'd never felt
this before. captivated by illuminating stardust.
recognizing the *god* in a woman.
praying this moment would never come to an end.
i was falling for the familiarity.
i was falling for the safety.
i didn't realize i was falling for myself.

volcanoes

creep
into these firm walls.
into this alluring cave.
into this heaven.

into everything you were ever promised.
into everything you've dreamed of.

creep.
into these flowers.
into this garden.
into this paradise.

into everything you've been missing.
into everything you need, love.

creep
into these fragile walls.
into this fractured space.
into this hell.

into everything i forgot to tell you.
into everything you could never even imagine.

creep.
into these volcanoes.
into this lava.
into this passion.

into everything we could've been.
into everything we never were.
into everything we could never be.

sometimes i feel alone.. even with you
my love, the one, who loves me most.
maybe i'm too much of a wanderer
always wondering what else is out there.
hoping i'm not missing much.
curious, yet guilty. thinking, you must not know me
all that well. i must have mentioned somewhere that
i'm not the type to settle. i'm not the kind of person
who will compromise forever. either you or me.
i will always pick me.

it wasn't until i was completely left empty,
after giving away every part of me,
that i realized only, i, could fulfill or drain me.
it wasn't until i was desperately waiting,
for promises that had no guarantees..
that i realized only, i, could ever save me.

i'm so intrigued with myself that i'm constantly
trying to figure me out.
i'm forever learning. even when i think i know it all,
i learn i don't.

a letter you'll probably never receive:

hey.. i know this is.. weird. probably the last time i'll ever reach out to you. and i know you're probably happy about that. i'm sorry. if i've ever been a burden or if i'm distracting you in any way. i don't mean to be. i just wanted to say sometimes when i'm faded i catch myself thinking of you. sometimes i think about us getting faded. sometimes i wonder if you ever got as high as me. and sometimes i wonder if you got higher. and sometimes i just wonder if you ever think of me. every time i listen to "guy" you come to mind. we always just chilled.. i wanna believe that i meant something to you but realistically.. i truly doubt it.
i'm really just reaching out to remind you that you're loved. or, for better words, "deeply cared for." i know some days you could use the love.
or whatever.

at some point, i became the kind of person
who falls in love with everyone.
i always find myself wanting to care
for everyone's heart.

i've let love destroy me.
i've let love make me question my existence.
i've let love almost kill me–
just to realize that this is not love.

hollywood hills

i keep going back to that night i was standing at
your doorstep wearing all white. or whoever's home
that was. all i know for sure is—i found comfort in
you. in that upstairs room, with that forestlike
view. i caught feelings for you at some point during
our nightly routine. where you faithfully called to
ask if i had smoked anything, and.. whether i had or
not—i still came to you. then i stayed for you. i
stayed a few hours longer than we ever intended for
me to.. but it always felt right. it wouldn't have made
any sense not to. but before i walked in that night i
was already full of love.. and conversation.
somehow i knew this would be the last time we saw
each other. somehow.. you knew too. i knew we were
better off as an idea or a fantasy or anything unreal
that wouldn't fuck me up or couldn't truly ruin me.
somehow you knew this was becoming something
bigger than just for fun so you pulled back. you kept
your distance. you held your own hands tight in
attempt to keep ours from slowly drifting. you held
your tongue all night in attempt to discipline your
instincts to keep from pursuing every single thing
that you've been missing.

i watched the hunger in your eyes.
i felt the empty in your bones. you looked at me and
said there was something you were missing. then you
asked if i was okay.. over and over again.
sometimes i wonder if it's because you weren't.
and sometimes i wonder if you aren't.

i keep going back to that conversation we had that
time we sat outside of your place or.. whoever's
haven that was. do you remember? i was wearing all
black. all i knew for sure was - you found the saving
you'd been craving in a woman you weren't used to
seeing. i was too busy trying to heal you to even feel
anything. and still you caught feelings for me at
some point during our nightly routine.. where you
spilled your heart hoping i was interested.. i promise
i was listening every time. one night you spoke about
me. you spoke about our souls and how it's a shame
that they were apart for so long. you spoke about
music and the way we make you feel. you said for so
long you'd been high on the wrong love and with
me - it feels like you're recovering. from a broken
spirit and a broken thing. you said you'd write about
me. you promised you'd write to me. for a while i
waited. i wanted so badly to believe that promises
weren't truly make-believe. still, i have yet to receive
anything and finally i've accepted how okay that is.

lately, i've been so focused on recovering
from several heartbreaks.
i've been listening to music more often. less of yours.
i've been falling in love with someone who makes
me feel like music. i've been focused on soul
connections. and i can't help but go back to those
nights and question myself about why i thought you
were "it" and if all those months were truly just
times wasted.

fools

i suppose we'll all end up mad..
preserving feelings for people who,
we decide, deserve our passion.
holding back our tongue from,
both, kissing and promises.
speaking, mainly, when spoken to.
weren't we made too intensely for this?
weren't we created too curious?
aren't we canny enough to know
we don't ever truly get to choose,
who comes and who goes?
haven't our hearts been broken enough?
haven't we more than a couple clues?

when? i wonder, might we start to believe..
that everything that's meant for us..
will always present itself as so.
when? i wonder, might we start to let go..
of everything we think we know.

maybe then, we'll begin to believe in ourselves.
maybe then, it'll all start to make sense.
maybe then, we'll truly be free—
to love.

switch your mentality from "i'm broken and
helpless" to "i'm growing and healing"
and watch how fast your life changes, for the better.

fillings

some people are temporary.
temporary fillers to make us happy
when we need it most. temporary
twilight zones. temporary bliss.
but some stick around to see you win.
some need you more than you need
them. some need you to temporarily
stick around to make them
happy—when they need it most.

so much freedom comes in the moment you realize that
everything you fall in love with is temporary.

at some point you'll realize that
your solitude is much healthier
than sharing space with
an uncertain person
who isn't meant for you.

do you ever think about love?
the idea of it?
like how incredible it is
to find people we want
to protect and hold
and heal forever?

how amazing is it to realize
we really don't get to choose
what happens to us?
we just have to deal
with whatever or whoever,
god brings us.

please,

don't come near me if you have no intention of
loving me. don't come near me if you have no plans
on touching me—the way you've never touched
another. don't come near me if you've felt this
before. or, if you've done this before. don't come
near if you're expecting something simple.
something temporary. something easy.
don't come near if you expect me not to love you,
the way i've never loved before. my love grows daily.
lately, i'm striving for "forever" type things.
don't come near if you expect me not to need you.
don't come near if you expect me not to feed you -
this passion. this emotion. this pain.
don't come near me if you expect not to stay -
in **love.**
in **we.**
in **trust.**

please,

don't come near me if you won't trust in us.
i don't want anyone similar to whom i'm used to.
i don't want anything i've done before.
i don't want anything temporary.
i don't want anything simple.

affairs

i've fucked you into loving me
with no intentions of anything serious.
i've helped you open up to me
just so i could see your pain.
just to give you a woman to remember–
every time you're in your head, and lonely.
or every time you need an example
of everything you're looking for.
i know you'll think back to me.
it's a shame i've learned your ways
or, your nasty habits i should say.
aren't i familiar to you?
don't i remind you of yourself?
don't you wonder where this pain came from?
don't you remember inflicting it within me?
i'm sorry i've returned the favor.
i'm sorry i can't be the one for you.

i've been a woman for some time now.
i no longer become attached to things
or, people who have no real purpose in my life.
and your purpose in my life
wasn't long-term or significant.
i'm sorry.. you thought otherwise.

i stopped being afraid of hurt when i saw i was only manifesting more hurt. the more energy u place in fear—the more reasons you'll receive.

to the men who broke my heart–
thank you.
if it weren't for you
my heart would have never had the opportunity to
become this strong.

we were never meant to be in love—
we were only ever meant
to learn love from one another.

discover what feeds you and then learn how to grow
it. water all that keeps you happy.

please, take care of your heart, spirit, and soul.
please, protect your happiness, energy, and mind.

don't you remember me from somewhere?
don't i look real familiar?
haven't i shown my face
plenty of times before?
haven't you seen my type?
haven't you tried..
and cried?
haven't you any clue
that i'm no good for you?
i ain't the answer you've been praying for.
you can quit searching here.
i got no trust left, to give.
i've got no truths left to tell.

i got nothing sweet for your
pride, or conceit.
i'm everything you've never wanted,
yet–everything you'll feel you ever need.
i'm not the one for you.
i'll fall short every time.
but you'll continue to choose me.
you'll say,
"ain't you the woman i said i loved before?
ain't you still mine?
ain't you tired of running?
ain't you ready to settle down?
damn, you still hurt from that?"

foolish boys

haven't you learned your lesson?
haven't you moved on?
haven't you any respect for me and my growth?
i know you don't mind that i'm preoccupied..
but i can no longer be here for you.
you should know better
than to try to make a fool of me.
things won't go your way this time around.

all women are not whole.
all women are not broken.
we are who we are—regardless
of how others are willing to accept us.
never be ashamed of your truth.

sacred wars

i'm challenging myself to do better. to dig deeper.
to love in a motherly way. to be as open-minded as
possible. to welcome in all of those who need me.
i'm afraid there's been a misconception. many
people are under the impression that women have
to be of some sort of value in order to be worth
loving. i'm here to say this is not true. you are
worthy of being loved in whichever form you come
in. whether that be half empty or half full. whether
that be beautiful on the inside or damaged. whether
you be optimistic, or pessimistic. there is no right or
wrong way to be a woman. don't allow someone's
idea of what a woman "is," or what a woman
"should be"–make you question yourself.
you *bleed* monthly.
there's a different kind
of magic in that.

grateful to the woman who believed in me.
said i was much more than a pretty face.
said i was too much of a poem to keep my mouth
shut. said i should talk more.

grateful to the men who've crushed me.
said i was too complicated;
just couldn't find the correct word for "complex."
said i was too damaged to be beautiful -
gave me a story to tell.

grateful to all the women who empowered
my broken ass to tell our story.

- *prayer* -

i've always had a unique relationship with god. i rarely speak about it because i'm always afraid people might take it the wrong way or might simply misunderstand me. although, that should be the least of my worries.. i can't help but care. i can't help but want to protect this union i feel i'm building from the ground up. this relationship, between a higher power and myself, started in my early teens. i was about twelve or thirteen when i decided i wanted to find out who, or what, "god" was. i wanted to learn and meet them for myself. or.. more so, i wanted to know how developing a relationship with one another could help me understand myself better. i wanted a spiritual partnership—similar to the one i had seen my father and god have. i also wanted to know why my mother never spoke much on the topic, but she always reminded me not to swear on "his" name. all i can remember thinking was, "i want to learn how to be this sacred." i wanted to be spoken of this highly. i wanted to know something that had become this sacred. i wanted to become the higher version of myself.

i started searching for churches to visit in my neighborhood and trying them all out. one after another, after the other. as soon as i felt a disconnect, or discomfort, i knew this wasn't the church or "god" for me. i, then, started searching for friends with churches. friends i thought highly of. friends i felt comfort in. i figured that if i couldn't find god on my own, i could find someone who has, or someone who could help me. i asked for help for so long that eventually, i'd given up. i forgot what i had even been searching for in the first place. then i remembered, to forget. i decided—i didn't need to be reminded of a feeling i'd never felt before. it wasn't until i was twenty-one that i discovered truth. the truth is, god doesn't have a safe house nor a hiding place. god just is. is a rose, is a scent, is an essence, is a cloud, is a tree, is a being. god lives in the midst of our being. god is a warning, a coincidence, a loss, a reason, a gain. god is the understanding of everything unconditional. you don't know love until you know unconditional. you don't know god until you know love.

truth lies beyond the word "god." the moment i found this understanding, i realized how intuitive i'd become to even allow myself to be guided, far, by spirit. i had been following paths that were led by the wind. i'd been living my life knowing, or assuming, that there was a love worth finding. so i went looking. what stood between god and me each time, was fear. i was afraid for too long. i was too afraid to lose myself. i was scared of letting go. i was scared to give so much "me" away that i'd forget to hold on to my sanity. sometimes, i'm still terrified. sometimes i still talk myself out of things. oftentimes, i wonder if i'm doing this life thing right, or if i'm doing enough, or if i could be doing more, or if any of what i'm doing is worth it. and by "worth it" i mean, worth the humility and the seclusion. i never feel sorry, or incomplete, or lost, even.. at times i just simply feel distant. i feel as though i've lost far too much time waiting for things that aren't meant for me. i've put my all into many relationships that still aren't clear. whether it be with others, with myself, or with god, or all three, simultaneously.

over time, i've found myself passionate about people who don't understand me, a great number of times, and so lately.. it's likely that i feel misunderstood more than ever. i don't speak up as often as i should because i'm afraid that i really don't make much sense inside anyway. i haven't expressed much in quite some time. it's been a while since i really allowed myself to feel deeply. i think i've forgotten how to. for a while i've just lived and loved above the surface. i've been trying to find my way out of depression's maze. i was high through most of it. i couldn't feel much.. but still, i tried.

i've made an enemy out of myself. i've suppressed my feelings. i've neglected many of my passions. i've, both, found and lost god due to being careless. i've developed quite an ego. i was so certain, for so long, that i was in this alone.

although, it was always me who rejected the help
i was given because i didn't care for the way i was
receiving it. i was too stubborn and unfamiliar.

i overlooked many of the signs lying amongst
the stars. i tried to make sense of each constellation,
but never truly could. i fought the universe's forces.
i missed out on god more often than i can count. i
would say i've missed out on many blessings, too,
if i didn't already know—you can never truly miss
out on things. i wanted to know god so badly, that
i spent years romanticizing the form in which "he"
would come. i deceived myself into believing that
god could or would come in only one form. i was
too heavily influenced by everything i'd been taught
along the way. but now i see the ways in which this
holy spirit has guided me, even when i did not know
it or when i could not tell.

recently, i decided i don't want any help, i
want to recognize god on my own—by the end of
this journey. i want to tap all the way within. i want
to dig deeper inside of myself and pull out every
weed i see. i want to be cleansed by the rain and
nourished by the sun and kissed by each breeze. i
want to plant a field of faith, trust, and reliance. i
want to invest my soul into an open conversation
that never ends. i want to change the idea of what
prayer looks like to what i personally feel it is. a
commitment. an exchange. communion and gospel.

my knowledge coincides with my
experiences. the places i've been, the people i've
exchanged love with, and each vice i've become
addicted to. i used to find comfort in others—now
i only wish to be alone more often. i only wish to
grow into my purpose. i want to be surrounded by
trees and water and divinity. nothing more.

the greatest part of my journey, thus far, is
learning that no matter what our ideas look like
in our heads and our hearts, we don't actually get
to decide how god will show up. we only get to
choose to trust our intuition when we feel a godlike
presence. for so long i lived my life with doubt
because i embraced god as man, even though she
has only ever presented herself as a woman for me.
for so long i was conflicted because i was intimidated
by my truth. i wasn't sure how i'd be perceived, but
finally, it doesn't matter. i don't care to be welcomed
for someone or something that i am not. i only pray
to be understood for trying to find peace within
myself.

now that i've let you in on my truth, i want
you to know that—i got you. but i won't always have
the answers you're looking for. there are answers
i'm still seeking. i won't always be the same person
you're looking for. there are parts of me, i'm still
missing. i pray we both learn to accept ourselves and
then one another. i pray we can remember to stay

focused on what matters most. this feels a lot like
a breakup letter but really it's a rebirth letter and a
prayer. it's a simple seed planted. it's our graduation.
i think our relationship will shape into something
much healthier. you and i and our trust with god.
whoever, she, or he, may be to you.

{still your mind.}

mother,
heal me.
cleanse me.
fill me.
help me.
save me.
protect me.
show me.
hold me.
trust me.
teach me.
guide me.
use me.
thank you.
i love you.

mother,

thank you.

thank you for everything that you are to me.
thank you for giving me another opportunity, day
after day. thank you for believing that i'm worth
another chance. thank you for all of your
unconditional love and support. i need you more
than i have expressed. i appreciate the openness of
our relationship. i aspire to come across others very
similar to me. others who are open, to any and
everyone, who will welcome me in regardless.
mother, i pray to be more open. with time i hope to
be, more and more, accepting of things and people
i've made a habit out of writing off—due to ego. i
pray to be less egotistical. i pray to be more free
with my decision-making. less calculated. less
organized. less structured. more in tune. more
impulsive. more driven by intuition. thank you for
holding my spirit in place whenever i need it most.
thank you for being patient with me. thank you for
waiting on me. to grow. to evolve. to develop into
the better version of myself
most fit for our relationship.

mother,

i can see your signs.

i feel them often, too.

i'm seeing the numbers thirty-three everywhere.

on license plates, receipts, oven clocks

and home addresses written into sidewalks.

do you prepare them for me a day in advance?

or do you give me more freedom than i know?

sometimes i can't tell

if i'm doing this with you or alone—

but i need you to know how good this feels.

the exchange.

the partnership.

the wholeness of our relationship.

there's an aura to it.

there's something extraordinary about connecting

with angels you have handpicked

and placed into my life.

i use them as guidance.

we are working together now.

there's something terrifying about the unknown,

still, i will never stray away.

i want to know my purpose,

so i'll keep going.

i won't give up until i know

you don't need me anymore.

but i pray we never outgrow one another.

mother,

please cleanse me.
free my body of pollution,
release all the poison,
empty my heart from delusion.
i want to start over.
help me abandon my worst habits.
open me up and repair my wounds.
clear my mind of harmful thinking.
i want to feel alive.
i'm exhausted.
i'm paying the price for not loving myself
more than i should have.
i don't blame you or anyone else even.
i just want to be freed.
i need you.

mother,

    fill my heart with purity.

    fill my heart with clarity.

    fill my heart with thanks.

    fill my heart with compassion.

    fill my heart with exception.

    fill my heart with forgiveness.

    fill my heart with courage.

    fill my heart with resilience.

    fill my heart with intention.

    fill my heart with honesty.

    fill my heart with acceptance.

    fill my heart with love.

    fill my heart with song.

    fill my heart with belief.

    fill my heart with positivity.

    fill my heart with happiness.

    fill my heart with passion.

    fill my heart..

mother,

i'm conflicted.

although i know where my heart lies, i don't know that i'm ever received the way in which i've prepared myself. i need help. i want guidance. i crave reassurance more than i should. i only pray for a still mind, these days. for a healthy mind. for a mentality that only adds to the people around me most. i needed to communicate with you because i feel misunderstood. i feel like my thoughts and feelings are too easily mistranslated. sometimes i feel too out of reach. sometimes i wish things made more sense. sometimes i wonder if my existence makes sense.

mother, i want to be received.

i don't know how. i don't know where.

i only know what it looks like to be transparent.

i wish to be more transparent.

i'm praying for transparency.

mother,

thank you
for allowing me to be transparent with you.
for listening before responding.
for showing me what it feels like to be
understood. for teaching me how to listen.
for helping me understand.

mother,

thank you for everything.
for protecting me, nurturing me,
developing me, forgiving me,
helping me, loving me, and trusting in me.
thank you for believing i'm worthy.

mother,

     thank you for not always giving me
everything that i want or ask for.

mother,

help me understand what it means to "love" myself.
and please, tell me that it's okay to be broken.
help me see how it feels to be loved
deeper than what i understand.
help me focus on the things that are important.
mother, help me perceive what is and what isn't of
importance. help me find myself.
please hold my hand until i'm found.

mother,

use me for your purpose.

guide me to your land.

to the promise of light.

to a love that's free.

listen when i say, i am yours.

hear me when i say, i love you.

forgive me if i have ever abused yours.

your love. your trust. your patience.

every day i am learning less about condition.

every day i am learning more about definite.

you make me complete.

i want to complete others.

i want to fill others.

i want people to feel you in me.

i want to bare my soul to any- and everything.

but, is this what you want for me?

have i got it mistaken?

have i no clue on what i think i should be doing?

mother,

save me from me. replace my memories.
i want to forget what i think i know.
liberate my ego. refresh my body.
i don't like it here. i don't make sense here.
i want to get away. i want to be alone.
i want to learn who i've become.
i want to learn how i've become, this.
i want to learn what it means
to *"become"* something beautiful.

i pray for the courage to see past my flaws
and acknowledge my strengths
and assets much more frequently.

mother,

keep me from any blocks i'm unaware of.
like enemies disguised as friends,
a religion that's misguiding,
a love that's temporary,
or any kind of distraction.
i don't want to continue to be naive.
please remove everything toxic to me.
please distance me from
those who don't root for me.
and from those who don't believe in me.
i want to find a heaven to feel safe in.
i want to create a community of passion.

mother,
i want to uplift and be
uplifted. i want to win just
as much as i want to
cheer for those who are
dear to me.

mother,

nowadays, i don't question what you have planned
for me, i just pray that i remain humble
through it all.

mother,
i pray that you remove all things
toxic to my development.
and i pray, to be both
trusting and understanding.

mother,
    protect my heart.
    give me the wisdom
    to know whom to keep close
    and whom to love from a distance.

when in doubt,
pray;
"i need you."

mother,
sorry if i ask for too much.
sorry if i give too little.

mother,
    please direct me in the path
    that does not allow me to settle.
    i'm tired of being unhappy.

i pray more now to understand,
than to be understood.
lately i've prayed to learn how to love,
rather than to be loved.

—improvement

mother,
grant me the courage to love again—after losing
love. help me acquire the desire to pick up all of my
heart's broken pieces, place them together, then,
please give me the courage to love harder.

pray for yourselves, then..
pray for all cities.
pray for all lives.
pray for all countries.
pray for universal peace.
we ALL need prayers.

the sun is my therapy.
the trees feed me energy.
i am loved by nature.
today, *i am love.*
there is no sense, only truth.

–this is my freedom song.

- rebirth -

i chopped off all of my hair while i was
in search of something. i was eager to unearth a
liberation i'd never known. i wasn't sure where
i would meet it; i just knew i was tired of feeling
weighed down. i looked up at god and heard her as
she encouraged me. occasionally, i wish there was
delilah to blame this on but i smiled at the moon
and let go, willingly. although, i created a story in
my head to inspire me. i pretended she was present.

delilah, and i, shared eyes and she
apologized as if this were her doing. i kissed her
shaking hands and reassured her that everything is
everything; which is really nothing at all, in reality.

"nothing deserves to be held on to forever"
i explained. "all things are meant to be outgrown.
and if they are meant to come back, they will in
better timing." as she frowned her face and looked
uncomfortable, i handed over the scissors. i watched
her take a deep breath, then i watched her hesitate.
at the moment i had no other legitimate explanation,
other than this was just another impulsive decision i
probably should have thought about for longer than
i did. finally, i closed my eyes; and a moment later,
i watched as my long curly blackish locks hit the
ground. one after another after another. i felt alone,
but calm.

directly afterward, i sat with myself in
silence. all other energies gone, all tales retired.. it

was just me and the stars. i looked up and searched for answers. i focused on one spot at a time, trying to figure out how i allowed myself to feel confined for so long. the entire time i stood there, i never could find the strength to speak. i didn't feel the need to express myself.

i just wanted to be. there were no tears worth shedding. there were no memories worth clinging on to. there was no one near to tell me i had officially gone mad. it was merely me and soundless space. my inner self felt lighter. my shoulders felt relieved. my body felt free. for once, in this moment, i felt completely at ease with the unknown.

with time, i've concluded that it wasn't the actual cutting of the hair that made everything exceptional, it was the detachment. it was the surrender. it was the sudden buoyancy my soul felt as each strand of hair on my head departed ways with me. it was the euphoric vibrations unfolding. it was my tranquil agreement with divorce that helped me see the light. it was the light at the end of this tunnel. it was the acceptance. it was the lesson that god has been trying to teach me. i had been holding on to resentment, grief, disappointment, regret, fear, and gloom—for longer than i could afford to. you see, the longer you hold on to things that aren't meant for you and your life—the longer you are a harm to yourself.

despite all the challenges i've faced and turmoil i've placed myself in, i'm learning to right my wrongs, let go of grudges, and forgive myself for all the damage i've done within. to those whom i've hurt along the way, throughout my journey, i'm sorry. you deserved better. despite our differences, i hope that from the chaos of our storm, or hurricane, you learned how to float above water. i hope you became much stronger. i hope you let your ill feelings pass. and finally, i pray you taught yourself how to trust again.

to the person i am still becoming: you are impressively human. you are graceful from the inside out. you are fragile yet resilient. you are so much bigger than you allow yourself to be. you are larger than any space you can't quite fit into. don't shrink your passions for the convenience of others. you don't deserve to treat yourself so harshly. you are a beating heart. you are an entire existence. i'm sorry if i've ever suffocated you and i'm sorry if i've ever avoided your truth or if i've convinced you that you aren't important. here are your wings, take them and fly. free your mind and keep rising;

this is your *rebirth*.

{forgive your past. move forward.}

the year obama left office

this year means a lot to me. it means i made it. it
means i stayed strong. it means i belong here. it
means i kept going, even if shit got too hard. it
means i got god with me. it means i got a purpose. it
means no matter how hard this life gets for me.. i
still make it through. i still survive. i still find a way
to wake up every day trying to find a reason to live
for. and some days i find that reason.
and some days i don't.

this year means i get a chance at this love shit. it
means i get a chance at this success shit. it means i
have an opportunity to take care of my parents if i
want it that bad. if i believe in myself enough. if i
understand the way this all works. this universe. this
manifestation shit. i'm starting to recognize my
power and so i'm starting to become more powerful.
i'm starting to see that i'm not "winning" in this rat
race.. but i'm elevating into a higher place. i'm
progressing. constantly. because i allow myself to.
because i give myself permission
to be happy
every day.

i give myself permission to be positive every day.
some days i fall short. but every day i'll continue to
allow myself to feel good if it feels right to. there
was a time when i wouldn't; or couldn't. i could
barely find beauty in life because i didn't feel
beautiful. i couldn't recognize beauty because i felt
like i had never really seen it. now i see it daily.
every day i'm falling more and more in love with
myself. i'm no longer in a place where i seek
validation or confirmation, that i'm worthy, from
someone else. i've learned to do that myself. this
year means i can finally say i love myself and mean
it. because no matter how ugly it gets?
i still choose to figure out myself.
this person.. who will never truly make sense.
but will always choose to try. one more time.
they told me a woman who cuts her hair is about to
change her life.
i can feel my life changing.

i am a battle always halfway between winning
and losing. i am always at war with myself. but,
for now, i am acknowledging that everything i've
gone through has been a million percent worth it.
my insides have never been this gorgeous.
my heart has never been so pure.

—abloom

it took me a while to recognize myself.
as mad,
as depressed,
and as exhausted as i'd become.
as content as i was.
aching come night,
ugliest by morning.
traumatized by inconsistency.
terrified of love.
terrified to love so hard
i end up lost.. again.
for a while,
i couldn't find myself.

i enjoy conversations with trees,
they each tell unique stories.
they wear patience so gracefully.
they remind me, that abandoned things
can still be beautiful.

the breath in your lungs is filled with god.

no-name poem

some poems don't have to have titles.
they just have to have meaning.. or hope.
they have to have more than enough
reasoning to universally grow.
they have to speak;
to more than just who's listening–
but also to those who won't.
those who love to present themselves as "whole."
those afraid to look broken,
or struggling.. to stay afloat.
some poems don't have to be in your face,
or begging, or forgiving.
some poems can just breathe.
just fulfill the spaces and places they're meant to be.
i'm okay with being that poem.
the no-name poem.
the behind-the-scenes poem.
the poem just meant for the people meant for me.
the poem brave enough to look crumbled.
the poem struggling.. to stay afloat.

i'd like to think that women are gods
because we resurrect men.
we lift them up so high they almost start to believe
they can live without us.

baptism

this morning i forgot my name.
i forgot the idea that my identity
holds weight.
i forgot to cleanse my face from the
night before,
i forgot to get rid of all the waste.
i forgot my dignity, my ego, and my
pride.
although, i remembered depression
dies there.
i keep forgetting to let go.
this morning i forgot that i was
broke.
i spend so much alone time with
trees,
i've found my power in watching
them burn
—then bleed.
sometimes, i think about the birds
and bees.
i wonder if—others realize—having
wings
doesn't mean to be free.

i'm still searching for honey
and all the good things
promised to me.
this morning i let my soul be.
tried to forget this thing called
"body."
tried to invite my friends to the
party–i forgot
no one really understands me.
this morning i forgot to be the
person people like me to be.
either quiet, graceful, or uplifting.
i forgot to be impressive.
i forgot to apologize for being
human.
how silly of us to forget how
inconsistent we can be.
mutually.
this morning i swore to god.
although, i really can't promise i
know him.
i can't remember the last time a
man saved me.

adam, then eve

there's a defect in my history
i've read an abundance of stories
about why i don't belong here.
there's a ruin in my foundation
i'm certain i was born this way
i've been crippled since before i can even
remember.
there's a monster in my house
i'm afraid it snuck in
at some point when i wasn't looking.
there's an enemy in my head
i can't seem to escape
she's unafraid to feed me poison.
i'm poisoned. i'm toxic.
i'm destroyed, internally.
there's a voice,
there's a force,
there's a curse,
there's life.
there's eve.
there's a being bleeding.
there's mary.
there's birth.

there is woman.

*sometimes we lose people because they don't want
to hear the truth about themselves and we're the
only ones who love them enough to tell them.*

for women who heal themselves:

your power lies in your tongue,
your eagerness to shout.
speak up more often,
you don't have to whisper or hum here.
you can show your grace, and your light,
and your magic all in the same breath—
you have our full attention.

believe me,
we can hear you.

we have seen you fall, then rise again.
the glisten in your eye, the heaven in your laughter,
your pliancy is heartening.
the weather is beautiful today, but
the rain is never too far away.
you influence god's decisions.
you uplift this world from, black and white,
to rainbows and love, with the wake of your smile.
you can reminisce on when shit was bad,
but things are better now.
you can free all of your worries, and sorrow,
and regret, and defeat,
you don't need it any longer.

you're much less a casualty,
more so a legacy.
look where faith has brought you.
you can love your body in the same breath
you pray for freedom.

—a word

acceptance

i'm tired of having to intersperse conversations with precaution and anxiety. i don't use my voice as often as i should. i'm trying to abandon my worry.
i haven't been as committed to my word as i should have been. i've been too concerned i might be judged. i'm fearful of love that is conditional. i know once i speak the truth i'll lose a lot of people who claim to be in my corner. ugly isn't always exceptional. but at times—i'm ugly.

have you ever
taken a second
to sit in space,
to sink
within yourself,
right where you are..
just to realize
how beautiful
it is to be alive?

unafraid to be woman

she wears her insecurities on her sleeves.
says "if you cannot add to me
i'd rather set you free."
she's alone often.
unafraid to be patient.
accustomed to being distant.
time caresses her silhouette—says,
"thank you for taking a chance on me.
i am on your side.
i am here to help you become whole."
she believes in her journey.
knows, it won't be easy
knows, she's not perfect.
knows being imperfect is okay.
she's unafraid
to risk.
she's unafraid
to fail.
she's unafraid
to be a woman.

i don't mind falling
and i don't mind loving
because i know what it's
like to not feel love
and i know what it's
like to not feel like love.
so i don't mind catching
your fall, either.

♡   fall with me—

what i will teach
my children:

1. love has no face. no religion. no color. no gender.
no conditions. no attachment. no requirements.
love will come, however it shall come.

2. you will not always win, and that's okay.
sometimes our greatest lessons are in the pit of
defeat. welcome each fall as an aide to flying.

3. your heart is your heart.
don't allow anyone to limit, discourage,
embarrass, or belittle you for feeling how you do.
express yourself.

4. there is a world out there that battles over ego.
set your ego free. free your heart again
and be the reason for peace
everywhere you are.

5. life is a journey, there is no rush to your
destination. wherever, whoever, that may be. be
patient. take your time.
find yourself first.

6. no one can validate you. you have to do that for
yourself. you have to constantly decide that
      you are more powerful than your adversities.

7. nothing is permanent. everything is temporary.
letting go and moving on will become a routine.
      and eventually, you'll be okay with that.

8. real love will find a way to you
when you are ready to become love.
when you are ready to let your guard down.
      when you are openhearted.

9. protect your dreams, goals, and desires.
nurture them with positive energy.
all things are possible
      when you truly believe in **you**.

10. there is nothing more effective than
conversation. open your mind to me. let me in on
how you feel. show me i'm wrong.
      help me, help you.

a reminder:
you are not broken;
you do not need to be fixed.
you need to grow into the kind of love
you wish to meet
then allow love to find you.

i'm a work in progress.
i'm still under construction.
whichever mistakes i make today
i pray i learn and grow from
but i'll never give up.

take a deep breath.
still your mind.
let all noise go.
bring it to tranquility,
even if it's for a second.
and thank god

—you're alive.

dear self,

i have good news, you're okay.
you're more okay than you've ever been.
some days it takes awhile, but..
you still manage to smile.
some days you feel helpless, even hopeless, but
you always find ways to fake it anyway.
fake conversations. fake laughter. fake teeth.
everyone loves it when you smile with your teeth.
more importantly..
in this moment,
you're "okay" enough to be able to fake it through.

there's so much life in that.

remember that time when you couldn't?
remember that time when you almost gave in?
you were always so much stronger..
after everything that you've been through -
things are finally coming together.
you are so inspiring,
you just keep going.
that's what makes you so admirable.
even when the entire world seems to be turning
upside down on you, you just keep growing.
you keep letting everyone know that you truly are
something *special.*

you.. in yourself are a poem.
i don't have to make you sound good.
i don't have to instill my hurt into you
to make you any more of a psalm.
i don't have to remind people that you've cried
on your knees begging god to
make things alright for once.
i don't have to fight for your recognition.
i don't have to warn anyone that you've made it,
despite all odds being against you.
you carry your bruises so gracefully.
no one doubts that you belong here.
you make life feel better,
for everyone.

all along i've been looking
and searching for
something or someone–
"beautiful" enough
to fall in love with.
all along i've
overlooked
myself.

i wanna be a lighthouse for others.
i want people to feel safe with me—
not because i want power over them,
but because i want to set us free.

i've got so many poems to write. both ugly and fair.
both—yearning for freedom.
i've fought this war plenty of times.
and many times, before, i've been defeated.
many times i forgot who i was.
i couldn't help myself find my way back.
couldn't make sense of it all.
this body i was all too unfamiliar with.
this heart that was much more of a burden.
both, beautiful and forgotten.
both, holy and hell.
can't lose again.
won't lose again.
trying,
to be more
in control.

if someone you let in,
comes in and damages you—
give yourself time
to recover.
repair.
regain trust
then love again
freely..
with no prerequisite,
and with no limits,
wholeheartedly.

i've been away for quite some time
i needed to get my mind right
writing on an empty heart,
backwoods and pipes
sage and prayer and trees.
i convince myself i do the natural thing.
i help myself go there.
just to hear myself speak.
something about the high,
something about the leaves
i can feel god here.
i can see her light.
i can find a reason convincing enough
to believe,
everything will
be alright.

—holy place(s)

you set the tone for every relationship
by showing others what you will
and will not tolerate.
don't let anyone take you for granted.

miss,

i'm dying to know your name..
i wish to know the pain
you've been through.
not to judge you
not to scold you
but to support you
in any way you need.
i know you've suffered,
i know you're hurting
i know you're tired of staying silent.
i know you're misunderstood.
please, open up.
please, let it out
please,
speak your truth
and give yourself
permission
to let it all go..

despite everything

that smile was her entire life.
always comforting when they need it most.
always showing up to break silence.
always brighter than a summer's day.
always masking the truth.
always hiding the pain.
always there; regardless.

a message from women:

do you know what it's like to be left alone in love?
do you know what it's like to feel stuck in love?
do you know what it's like to be too depressed?
do you know what it's like to have to beg for
forever from a person who neglects your history?
do you what it's like to lose everything?
do you know what it's like to feel abandoned?
do you know what it's like to wait?
do you know that i will never be
too near or too far away?
honestly, i'm still waiting for closure.
i still question what this is—or what this was
because i can't help but hope
our feelings were mutual.
do you know how it feels to constantly chase
a feeling you're addicted to?
do you know i've got the jones for you,
and an appetite, and a sweet tooth?
do you know i prayed for you?
from night till day;
regardless of my better judgment or dismay.
time after time after promises that never
seemed impossible or too good to be true.
do you know what it's like to try convincing
yourself that—this was the truth.

like i was the woman created for you.
do you know how much i've craved you?
i've searched for you everywhere
in *people,* in *prayer,* in *psalm,*
in different lovers, in god.
and god—i, wish you really knew
that i'd love you till death,
or that i'd kill for you.
or that i feel you, like soul deep, like
deeper than anyone ever will.
do you know what it's like to feel dead inside
and see you so alive, still?
but these days i feel alive.
i've been able to realize that
you just weren't meant for me.
these days i don't cry over
spilled milk,
or lost love,
or things i have no control of.
these days i just love myself more.
i just know there's a happily ever after.
these days i just—don't see it with you.
nothing personal i think i just fell too quick
for your potential.
i just wanted you to be the one.
i just thought we made sense

but now i love myself enough to know better.

no in between

my heart has never been lukewarm.
either on fire or freezing. healing or bleeding.
never not fighting for peace; or waiting and hoping
for some kind of rescuing. rescue from bruise.
rescue from pain. rescue from hurting.
rescue from me. *rescue from especially me.*
finally learning i'm my biggest enemy.
i hurt me most.
i'm just trying to find a space
where i can breathe better.
where i can be better.
i'm trying to be less cold.
trying to be more passionate
about everything and
everyone around me.
trying to burn more often.
trying to find a space
where i'm okay more often.
where i'm high more often.
where i'm fully loved.
trying to be in a place where
my heart doesn't accept anything
less than pure happiness
coming from others—
but also, coming from, especially, me.

by no means am i fearless,
i'm just as scared as you..
i just know fear poisons love—
so i choose to be alive.
if that means to be brave,
so be it.

took me years to
appreciate
my "softness."
and my heart.
and my love.
and my craving
for a love
that i deserved,
from a love
who deserved me.

acknowledge your growth.
honor your healing.
don't find yourself back
at where it hurts the most.
keep moving forward.

requirements

i'm not attracted to anyone who isn't excited about
me. i want to be shown love consistently. i want to
be shown off, celebrated, and reminded of my
beauty. i don't want to surround myself around
anyone who doesn't make me feel anything. i want
my presence craved anytime i go missing. i want my
spirit full in return of me giving you everything. the
way i love is everything but ordinary.
the way my heart is set up, i fill people until i'm left
empty. unintentionally, i will shower you with all of
me until i'm left with nothing. all i want is for
someone to feel what i feel and love how i love.
someone who's eager to give me mutuality–
without me having to question whether or not
they're meant for me.

depths of desire

i don't want to leave you speechless,
i want you to open up and engage with me.

when a person truly loves you, they search for cracks to fill, within you. they never make you feel guilty for not being whole.

we are not our parents.
or their mistakes.
or our mistakes.
we are everything that
each mistake—learned from,
has made us.

    —accept your being

i'm grateful to have woken up
happy and healthy this morning.
to me, that is enough.

kehlani's intro

my condolences to anyone who's ever lost me
and to anyone who got lost in me
or to anyone who ever felt they took a loss with me.
my apologies.
for the misunderstanding or the lack thereof.
i'm sorry you missed the god in me.
and i'm sorry you missed the light.
i'm sorry you forgot the way i arose like the moon,
night after night.
with the burden to forgive
eager to feed you everything.
see.. i'm a holy woman.
i know what it's like to give life to a being
without ever needing to press skin
against one another.
i've practiced how to hold my tongue long enough,
i'm afraid i forgot to say goodbye.
i'm afraid you're under the impression that i was
made to please you.
i was under the impression,
you understood me better.

the truth is,
i'm a super woman.
and some days i'm an angry woman.
and some days i'm a crazy woman.
for still waiting..
for still loving harder even if i'm aching.
for still trusting that i'm still worth the most.
for still searching
for someone to understand me better.

|

i was never meant to be "enough" for anyone.
i serve no purpose fulfilling the desires of others
through any expectations. i am here for me.

i wanna go to nirvana with you.
i want you to volunteer to be my partner.
i want a hand to hold.
i want to be the reason your face glows.
i wanna fill your mind with
cloud nine and euphoria.
i want you to see my vision more clearly;
i want roses around the bed
and vases filled with white or pink lilies.
i want you to touch every flower.
i want you to pluck all my petals.
i want you to climb in love with me.
i want strawberries and grapes,
just for aesthetic purposes.
i wanna fill you, love.
i wanna feel you feel my love.

another way to say
i love you;

i've always believed "you are who you attract" but
every day i wonder if the universe made a mistake. i
wonder if i make sense for you. i wonder if our
connection keeps us in sync.. despite the areas in
which i fall short. i look at you in the highest light
and hope that you know this. you help me reach my
full potential, and for that i'm forever grateful. you
remind me to love myself, and for this i will forever
love you. i try to write you into my story, again and
again, but the words never form for me. sometimes i
wonder if it's because i never write about people
who are too good to be true.. or if it's because our
love is too complex, too sacred, too holy.. or maybe
i'm just not used to writing about happiness.. or
maybe for once my heart knows the meaning but
my mind hasn't processed it yet. or maybe the
reality is you are a blessing. i promise to never forget.
you make me better.
you make me forget what love isn't.
you make me proud to say i'm yours.
every day i pray for you.

au courant

i love who this person has become.
she loves herself enough
to truly love others.

never be afraid to look yourself in the mirror,
with a broken heart and a bruised spirit..
to tell yourself
"i need you."

- *closing letter* -

as we are at the end of this psalm, i want to encourage you to listen to your heart more. i hope you discover the freer side to life. i'm praying for your happiness. i want you to reread this as many times as you need to. and, **every time**, i want you to find a new understanding. i want you to find the beauty within yourself, then i want you to believe in all the ideas that your mind is sitting on. your thoughts are more powerful than you think. your voice is a force. do not be too frightened to use it. if i can do it, so can you.

a reminder: you are loved. you are love. i have faith that one day you'll never forget this. give yourself time. give yourself space. give yourself more credit, you will find the way. you will find the light. never forget to pray—and instead of having expectations, just be patient and wait. the answers come when the mind is clear. soon enough, everything you've ever gone through will make sense. and when it finally does, you will learn how to use this new awareness to move and think in ways that are beneficial to you and your purpose. you will find alignment.

i want you to learn the truth about who
we are as a people. we are fragile. we are curious.
we are emotional. we are afraid. we, individually,
are so fucking fascinating. look at yourself. look
at how human you are. look at how delicate your
skin is. look at how fast your heart still beats when
you've found love. look at how much you've grown.
look beyond the surface. look at your spirit. look at
how great of a team you make with one another.
thank yourself. thank the stars. credit the moon for
comforting you when no one else could. you ever
notice how bright the moon shines for you some
nights? look at the bigger picture. look how that shit
from last year doesn't even matter anymore. look
at how you survived. look at the way your wounds
are fading to black and white. look at how we did
it together. look how invested we are. this is how
relationships are supposed to look. this is how love is
supposed to be. healthy, free, and unapologetic.
look at how graceful you are.
look at how strong you've become.

—isn't this something to thank god for?

Andrews McMeel Publishing
a division of Andrews McMeel Universal
1130 Walnut Street, Kansas City, Missouri 64106

www.andrewsmcmeel.com

18 19 20 21 22 BVG 10 9 8 7 6 5 4 3 2 1

ISBN: 978-1-4494-9383-7

Library of Congress Control Number: 2017959256

Editor: Patty Rice
Art Director: Julie Barnes
Production Editor: David Shaw
Production Manager: Cliff Koehler

Find Reyna on Twitter @DearYouFromWe
Find Reyna on Instagram @ReynaBiddy
Find Sara on Instagram @SaraFaber_

ATTENTION: SCHOOLS AND BUSINESSES
Andrews McMeel books are available at quantity discounts with bulk purchase for educational, business, or sales promotional use. For information, please e-mail the Andrews McMeel Publishing Special Sales Department: specialsales@amuniversal.com.